KANSAS SPIRIT

15 HISTORICAL QUILT BLOCKS
& THE SAGA OF THE SUNFLOWER STATE

By Jeanne Poore

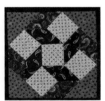

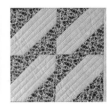

KANSAS CITY STAR BOOKS

KANSAS SPIRIT
Fifteen Historical Quilt Blocks
& the Saga of the Sunflower State

By Jeanne Poore

Editor: Evie Rapport

Technical Editor: Jane Miller

Design & Illustrations: Brian Grubb

Photography: Aaron Leimkuehler

Historical Photographs and
Illustrations: The Kansas City Star and
the Kansas State Historical Society

Technical Illustrations: Gary Embry

Production Assistant: Jo Ann Groves

Published by Kansas City Star Books
1729 Grand Blvd.
Kansas City, Missouri 64108
All rights reserved.
© 2006 by The Kansas City Star Co.

ON THE COVER:
Flying Around Kansas
by Joan Streck

First edition, second printing
ISBN 10: 1-933466-19-7
ISBN 13: 978-1-933466-19-4

Library of Congress Control Number:
2006932560

Printed in the United States
by Walsworth Publishing Co.,
Marceline, Missouri.

To order copies, call StarInfo at
(816) 234-4636 and say "Operator."

www.PickleDish.com

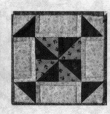

KANSAS SPIRIT

TABLE OF CONTENTS

ACKNOWLEDGMENTS

First, I would like to express my gratitude to my family for their support and encouragement of my love of quilting and for their patience when my designing, creating, teaching, lecturing and writing take time away from them. They are always with me in spirit.

I thank the Kansas Quilters Organization and Golden Oldies for sharing their knowledge of quilt making not only with me but also with all members of their group. They have expanded my horizons. Special thanks to the wonderful ladies whose works are included in this book. They kept the faith that it could and would be done. I also want to add my thanks to members of the other guilds and small quilt groups to which I belong. You know who you are and how much I appreciate all of you.

Thank you, Carol Kirchhoff, owner of Prairie Point Quilt shop in Shawnee, for friendship and support in my projects. She and the entire staff are always available to help with ideas and plans as well as to challenge me to do my best. Working in such a creative environment is fun and stimulating.

Special thanks to Evie Rapport for her copy editing and attention to details. She also kept us on schedule. I wish to thank Brian Grubb for his innovative graphic designs and illustrations, and for having such good friends who allowed us to take photos in their homes. Thanks to Aaron Leimkuehler for his photography skills. I thank my technical editor Jane Miller for stepping forward when needed and Gary Embry for his technical illustrations. I also thank Jo Ann Groves, production assistant, and a special thanks to Doug Weaver for the opportunity to share the Kansas Spirit quilt story with readers.

KANSAS SPIRIT

15 HISTORICAL QUILT BLOCKS
& THE SAGA OF THE SUNFLOWER STATE

Dear Quilt Enthusiasts,

Some of us are native Kansans, and some of us are transplants, but most of the members of the Kansas Quilters Organization are proud of the spirit and heart of Kansas.

KQO began in 1984 when a group of people decided it was time to create a statewide organization of like-minded quilters. From the first organizational meeting at Rock Springs Camp, it was clear that the desire to create and share ran deep in each of us. Our meetings always involve instruction, inspiration, fellowship, friendship and food. We have no set place to meet, as the diversity of the state is a natural resource.

KQO has 21 hard-working board members serving three-year terms. Our interests and areas of expertise are varied, but we all have a hand in creating a couple of great events every year.

More information on KQO can be found on our Website, www.ksquilters.com. Check us out. We adore old friends, but we also get really enthusiastic about making new friends. We hope you enjoy this book of Kansas memories, Kansas fabrics and Kansas quilters.

Happy Quilting,

Nancy Austin Swanwick
KQO President 2004-06

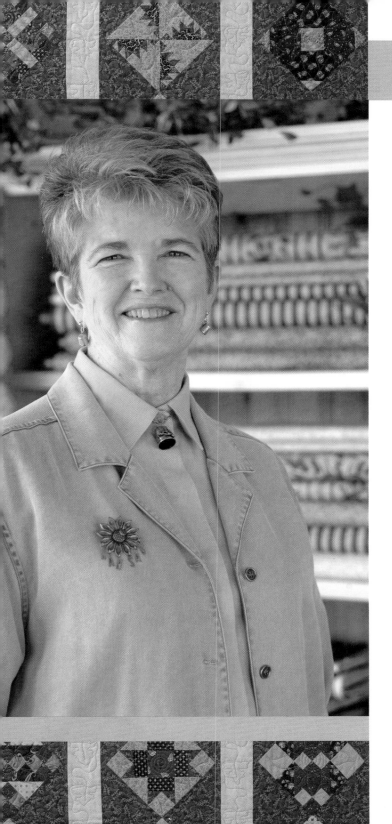

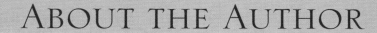

ABOUT THE AUTHOR

Jeanne Poore describes herself as an old-fashioned, traditional quilt maker whose personal history includes grandmothers and a great-grandmother who quilted and shared their knowledge and love of the craft with her.

Although she has worked in tax offices, accounting firms and insurance companies and has coordinated training seminars for a computer software company—what her husband calls "real jobs"—she never gave up her quilting. She has worked and taught at Prairie Point Quilts in Shawnee since it opened in June 1995 and has designed the shop's Block-of-the-Month program since it started in 2002.

An international lecturer and teacher, Jeanne also has written about quilts in numerous books and in such magazines as *Quilting Today, Traditional Quiltworks, Old Fashioned Patchwork* and *Better Homes and Gardens Quilt Sampler.*

The book *Star Quilts—The Legendary Kansas City Star Quilt Patterns*, published in 1999 by the Kansas City Star Co., features patterns redrafted by Jeanne. Also in the Star quilt series, Jeanne's redwork book *Santa's Parade of Nursery Rhymes* was published in 2000, and *Fan Quilt Memories* came out in 2001. Her work has been featured in *Celebrate the Seasons With Quilts, Kansas City Quiltmakers, Quilters' Stories, Hearts and Flowers, Quilt and Embellish in One Step* and *Horn of Plenty.*

She has been active in local, state and national quilting organizations since the mid-1980s and has served as an officer and on boards of directors. She quilts weekly with the Legler Barn Quilters at the historic Legler Barn Museum, and she designs patterns for piecing under the name Jepo Designs.

She was born in her maternal grandparents' farm home in Washington County, Kan., and raised in Kansas City, Kan. She has lived in Overland Park since 1966 with her husband of 45 years. They have a son, Darryl, and daughter-in-law, Debbie; and a daughter, Natalie, and son-in-law, Rick. They are blessed with four wonderful grandchildren, Daniel, Krista, Kayla and Rachel. All of Jeanne's family have quilts made to commemorate special occasions in their lives.

KANSAS SPIRIT

HOW THE PROJECT WAS BORN

In June 2003 a group of 21 past and present members of the board of the Kansas Quilters Organization — who call themselves the Golden Oldies — met for one of their regular retreats, this time at the historic Buckeye School north of Hays.

"The Spirit of Kansas" was the theme for that retreat's project. Blocks with particular Kansas roots were incorporated, and everyone was encouraged to use fabrics by Kansas designers Barbara Brackman, Terry Thompson and Lynne Hagmeier.

Frances Shearer was the hostess. Those in attendance were the late Fern Bentz, Diane Bradbury, Jeannine Bryan, Pam Calhoun, Doris Callaway, Barbara Doze, Dawn Habiger, Jean Hamilton, Linda K. Headings, Dixie Horton, Nadine L. Mehl-Martinitz, Leanna Mohr, Tony Muñoz, LaRue Nuest, Betty Piester, Gwen Rankin, Joan Streck, Nancy Austin Swanwick, Cathy Zahn and Jeanne Poore.

One particularly fine quilt born of that project was Joan Streck's Flying Around Kansas, which won the Grand Champion Best of Show Purple Ribbon at the Kansas State Fair in 2005. Other examples of large and small quilts begun that weekend are part of this book.

The Kansas Quilters Organization was formed in 1984 at Rock Springs Camp near Manhattan. The first 21-member board of directors wanted to promote and protect historical quilt collections, especially by documenting quilts that were in more than 200 museums in the state. The first board contacted these museums either by letter or in person.

In 1996, Carol Elmore was asked by the board to resume the project. She and her committee members—Cathy Zahn, Joan Streck and Linda Frihart— began a dialogue on what could be done with information gathered from around the state. Kathrine Schlageck of the Marianna Kistler Beach Museum of Art at Kansas State University in Manhattan also was interested in doing a similar project. The KQO board agreed to donate money to the Beach Museum and to give Kathrine access to the guild's files on quilts in Kansas museums. The 1999 book *Sunflower State Quilts* was the result.

The KQO meets twice a year, once in June and again in the fall, usually October. Every second year they have a three-day retreat. They have met in towns and cities throughout the state: Hays, Colby, Norton, Phillipsburg, Seneca, Emporia, Great Bend, Liberal, Hutchinson, Salina, Sterling, Lindsborg, Ottawa, Paola, Olathe, Pittsburg, Parsons, Manhattan, Dodge City, McPherson and Lawrence. The sessions include lectures, workshops, block exchanges, vendors and fun events. The board of directors gets together four times a year to organize the meetings.

The guild supports the Kansas State Fair's quilt program, promotes the craft through its Quilter's Day Out events throughout the year all around the state, and holds fellowship training classes every other year as part of its educational commitment.

From KQO members, the Kansas Golden Oldies was formed. The group comprises present and past board members who wish to continue to share their interest in quilting and fellowship by meeting annually. The first Golden Oldies gathering was held in Atwood, hosted by Caroline Peterson Searles. The group has since met in Bird City, Salina, Winfield, Hays, Paola, Greensburg, Arkansas City and Emporia.

'FINDING THE BEAUTY'

When George R. Pasley saw Joan Streck's champion quilt Flying Around Kansas at the state fair in Hutchinson, he was so impressed that he wrote a column about it for the *Pratt Tribune* on Sept. 15, 2005. It was, he said, "beautifully done and truly Kansas." What impressed him even more than the blocks and their setting and the fabrics she chose was the twining pattern she used for the quilting: Sunflowers and Bindweed.

How his Uncle Phil and other farmers would have sneered about beautifying those weeds! How many hours had they spent trying to root them out of valuable grazing and farming land?

Pasley had to laugh, but then, he said, "Maybe the quilter had the last laugh. After all, the people of Kansas have been finding the beauty in what we find where we live as long as we have lived in Kansas. So, if beauty can be found in Indian hatchets, whirlwinds, Kansas dugouts, and even Kansas troubles, then surely it can be found in sunflowers and bindweed."

These friends, separated in age by more than 40 years, came together through their involvement in the Kansas Quilters Organization. Their combined years of service to the group total more than 325, their service on the board 115 years and their experience quilting more than 685 years. When you consider all that history, expertise and creativity, it is no wonder that the art of quilting is alive and flourishing in Kansas.

■ FERN BENTZ SALINA

Fern was a registered nurse who worked at the Asbury Hospital in Salina. She hand quilted for other people during her nursing career and after she retired. She enjoyed taking quilt classes and attending quilting events. She never bought more fabric than the required amount for a project, so she did not have a stash.

Fern, who died in March 2005, was a member of KQO for 19 years and served as secretary.

■ DIANE BRADBURY WINFIELD

Diane began quilting in 1990, when she quit teaching school at Oxford, Kan. She notes that her aunt can remember her great-grandmother sitting by a wood-burning stove in the evening sorting her quilt scraps, which she kept in a shoebox. Diane's mother also made a number of quilts, sometimes making new tops to put over worn quilts.

Diane joined KQO in 1991 and served on the board for six years. She says, "The Golden Oldies retreat is something I look forward to each summer."

■ JEANNINE BRYAN BURDEN

Jeannine, a retired schoolteacher, is a member of several quilt guilds. Her mother quilted until she was 90 years old, and her grandmother was also a quilter. Her favorite blocks from the Kansas Spirit quilt are the Dugout, because her great-grandparents lived in a dugout near Saffordville; and the Whirlwind, because her husband was caught in a tornado and survived without a scratch even though the hay barn he was near was destroyed.

She has been a member of KQO for 14 years, serving on the board for six years.

■ PAM CALHOUN HUTCHINSON

Pam, who is currently a controller at a data center, has worked in accounting for 33 years. She says her great-grandmother was a quilter, both her grandmothers were quilt-top makers, and she taught her mother to hand quilt. The blocks that remind her of her heritage are the Dugout and

Courthouse Steps, because her paternal grandfather lived in a soddie for a short time and he was also a probate judge in Rush County for 20 years. The Corn & Beans block represents her grandmother's garden, and Pam likes the State Fair Sunflower, which she said looked hard but really wasn't.

She has been a member of KQO for 19 years, serving on the board for six years and as president for two years.

■ DORIS CALLAWAY GARDEN CITY

Doris' mother taught her to quilt when Doris was 12 years old and living in Protection, where she later taught quilting classes. She is a fifth-generation quilter: Her mother and dad both quilted, as did her grandmother, great-grandmother and great-great-grandmother. She says her mother was born in the dugout home where her grandparents lived.

She has been a member of KQO for 19 years, serving on the board for six years, and was president in 1995.

■ BARBARA DOZE RUSSELL

Barbara retired from 25 years as a speech pathologist in schools before taking up quilting. Although a latecomer to the craft, she has made numerous quilts for her family and won a county Grand Reserve on her Trip Around the World quilt. She also enjoys knitting, which she says is from her Brownie Scout days.

She joined KQO in 1994 and served on the board for six years.

■ DAWN HABIGER KALVESTA

Dawn, a farmer and rancher, is a third-generation quilter whose grandmothers and mother all quilted. She made her first quilt at age 10 along with her younger brother, Tom Reed, who was 5, because their grandmother Emma Stiawalt challenged them to do so. They both have their first quilts.

She has been a member of KQO for 18 years and served on the board for two years.

■ JEAN HAMILTON SALINA

Jean was taught to quilt by her husband's aunt and has quilted for 50 years. She has lived and worked in 15 towns in Kansas and four other states because of her husband's frequent transfers. Jean's quilt titled Kansas Krafts Kquilt was in an exhibit that traveled to various museums in the state for Kansas' 125th anniversary.

She is a charter member of KQO and served on the board for six years.

■ LINDA K. HEADINGS **HUTCHINSON**

Linda, who has been a nurse for 30 years, and her husband have lived on what she calls "the home place" outside Hutchinson for 24 years. Her grandmother gave her quilt blocks to embroider, and her mother helped her finish them into a quilt in 1976. However, she did not take a quilt class until 1984.

She has been a member of KQO for 19 years and is currently the secretary. Her favorite block is the Sunflower.

■ DIXIE HORTON **HAYS**

Dixie retired as the executive director of Sunflower Girl Scout Council after 26 years with the organization. Her mother and grandmother were quilters. She says her daughter is not a quilter, but two granddaughters have already taken it up.

She has been a member of KQO for 12 years and served on the board for six years. She was co-editor of the "KQO Quarterly Newsletter" with Frances Shearer for two years, then editor for six more years.

■ NADINE L. MEHL-MARTINITZ **SALINA**

Nadine, a bookkeeper and secretary, was 10 when her grandmother first let her sew squares together on her treadle sewing machine. When her children were away at college, she took her first quilting class and has been addicted ever since. Her favorite blocks were the State Fair Sunflower and Kansas Troubles. She said the most challenging block was Corn & Beans.

She has been a member of KQO for 17 years and served on the board for six years.

■ LEANNA MOHR **WAKEENY**

Leanna, the office manager for a chiropractor, is married and has a daughter and grandson. She grew up a tomboy on a farm south of Wakeeny and loved the outdoors. When she saw a quilt show on TV, she was hooked. She went to the quilt shop in Hays and was asked to visit the local Big Creek Quilt Guild. She has been an active member now for 16 years.

She has been a member of KQO for 15 years and served on the board for 2 years.

■ TONY MUÑOZ **PARSONS**

Tony has retired from teaching school after 32 years. He has quilted for 25 years and is the only one in his family who has quilted. He decided to name his quilt Frijoles Fritos Con Chile Verde (Fried Beans With Green Pepper) after making the Corn & Beans block.

He is a charter member of KQO and served on the board several times, for 18 years in all, and has been president two years.

■ LA RUE NUEST HUTCHINSON

LaRue is a retired teacher at the high-school and community-college levels. She is a fourth-generation quilter, but she made her first quilt in 1982 for a new grandchild. She has since become an appliqué quilt instructor in her hometown. She has taken classes from 21 appliqué teachers to continue to learn all she can about her favorite quilting technique. Her favorite block from this project was the State Fair Sunflower.

She wants to quilt for the rest of her life and be buried with her sewing machine, thread and lots of fabric. She said, "I heard that in heaven your bobbin never runs out of thread."

LaRue is a charter member of KQO and served on the board for six years and as president for two years.

■ BETTY PIESTER COATS

Betty, who lives on a ranch southwest of Pratt, was the postmaster of the Belvidere Post Office and retired in 1993. Although her mother was a quilter, Betty did not start quilting until 1986 when she took a class from Doris Callaway. Like several other members of the Kansas Quilters Organization Golden Oldies, she and her family survived a tornado.

Betty has been a member of KQO for 16 years and served on the board for four years.

■ GWEN RANKIN MINNEOLA

A school-bus driver and rancher, Gwen learned quilting from magazines and books until joining KQO, because the closest quilt shop was 50 miles away. Her grandmother quilted but had quit by the time Gwen started. One of her favorite blocks is the Dugout because she remembers her Grandfather Yunker telling her about moving out of their cramped, dirty dugout to a wooden house with floors and windows. The cows were moved into the dugout until the middle of the winter, when the cows were ejected and the family moved back into the warm dugout—dirt and all.

Gwen says she remembers the Kansas Spirit weekend as a blur of laughter and piles of fabric, one of her favorite memories of all time. Good friends, food, sewing and laughter—how could it get any better?

She has been a member of KQO for six years, on the board four years.

■ FRANCES SHEARER HAYS

Frances, co-owner of Tumbleweed Crossing Quilt Shop in Hays, was a schoolteacher, worked for the Girl Scout Council 15 years and was executive director of CASA in Hays for four years. Her mother, grandmother and great-grandmother were quilters. She did some quilting in the 1970s and purchased her first long-arm machine in the 1980s.

She has been a member of KQO for 12 years and served on the board for six years, two years as president.

■ JOAN STRECK OVERLAND PARK

Joan has been quilting since 1969. Both her grandmothers quilted, but she did not start until after their deaths. Among the things she inherited were quilt tops and unfinished quilts. Since she had been sewing most of her life, she decided she could finish the quilts. She started by trial and error, and the choice of fabrics and books was limited at the time. After taking one class at a newly opened quilt shop, she was hooked, and she still takes classes whenever possible.

She says her favorite block is Kansas Beauty, because, she says, "If you take the time to really look at the scenery in all the seasons, Kansas is a beautiful state."

Joan has been a member of KQO since the late 1980s and served on the board for six years.

■ NANCY AUSTIN SWANWICK FORT SCOTT

Nancy is a schoolteacher who was raised in her family's store, Kirk Austin's Fabrics in Parsons. She taught food classes for more than a decade and is now enjoying teaching quilting construction and design to students at Fort Scott High School. She likes variety and movement in her quilts and says she has many projects going at once. Her favorite block is the Sunflower, but she also likes the Maple Leaf.

A charter member of KQO, she has been on the board for four years and is currently president for the second year.

■ CATHY ZAHN BURDETT

Cathy is a special-education teacher. She learned to quilt and sew with her grandmother, using a treadle sewing machine—always a challenge, she says. She still has the 9-patch quilt they made together.

She has been a member of KQO for the 10 years without interruption and had belonged previously. She was vice president in charge of planning several of the state meetings. Her Kansas quilt is still a work in progress.

This block, also known as Autograph, represents the centennial of the state of Kansas, which joined the union on Jan. 29, 1861. *(See the Kansas Star block for more historical details.)*

Many of the settlers who came to the Kansas Territory after it was established in 1854 were committed to the pro-slavery or abolitionist political movements. But many also came for the land. Under the provisions of the Preemption Act of 1841, an individual could claim up to 160 acres—a quarter-section of land—and, after a period of residence, could buy it for $1.25 an acre.

The passage of the Homestead Act in May 1862, one the most important pieces of legislation in U.S. history, opened to private citizens more than 270 million acres in the public domain—much of it in the Louisiana Purchase of 1803.

Homesteaders who were at least 21 years old and head of a household could claim 160 acres of land. They had to live on the claim, build homes and make other improvements, and farm the land for five years; they could then own the claim after paying a filing fee of $18. More than 29,000 claims were made in Kansas by 1871.

ROTARY CUTTING FOR 6" BLOCK

TAN BACKGROUND
1—4 1/4" square, subcut diagonally twice to get 4 large triangles
4—2" squares for corners

LARGE RED PRINT FOR CENTER
1—2 5/8" square

BLACK PRINT
4—1 5/8" x 2 5/8" rectangles

SMALL RED PRINT FOR STAR POINTS
4—2" squares, subcut diagonally to get 8 triangles

ROTARY CUTTING FOR 12" BLOCK

CREAM BACKGROUND
1—7 1/4" square, subcut diagonally twice to get 4 large triangles
1—4 3/4" square for center

TAN PRINT FOR CORNER SQUARES
4—3 1/2" squares

RED PRINT
4—2 5/8" x 4 3/4" rectangles

GREEN PRINT FOR STAR POINTS
4—3" squares, subcut diagonally once to get 8 triangles

Nadine L. Mehl-Martinitz

L: *Joan Streck*
R: *Nadine L. Mehl-Martinitz*

■ Stitch 2 star point triangles to adjacent sides of a corner square (#1). Press toward the corner square. Make 4 of these units.

Stitch these units to the rectangle (#2). Press toward the rectangle.

Stitch the large background triangles to opposite sides of 2 of the units (#3). Press toward the background triangles.

1

2

3

■ Stitch 2 (#2) units to opposite ends of the center square. Press toward the center square.

■ Stitch the remaining side units (#3) to the opposite sides of the center strip, matching the intersecting seams. Press toward the center unit again.

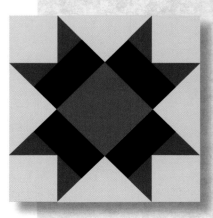

PIONEER SPIRIT   Pam Calhoun

INDIAN HATCHET

Kansas derived its name from the Native American Kansa tribe, often translated as "South Wind People" or "Wind People." The Kansa tribe was a branch of the Osage, the largest Indian nation of the southern Sioux tribes and the most powerful and wealthy at the time of the Louisiana Purchase in 1803.

The tribe's experience in Kansas includes fierce warfare with the Cheyenne, Pawnee and Sauk as well as with the Kiowa, Comanche and others. Kansas was also the home of the Arapaho, the Plains Apache, Cherokee, Iowa, Kiowa Apache, Wichita, Delaware, Chippewa, Kickapoo, Miami, Muncie, Sac, Fox, Pawnee, Pottawatomi, Shawnee and Wyandot/

Huron tribes. Many of these tribes had moved or been relocated from the Ohio River Valley and other eastern regions in the 19th century.

This pattern name was listed in the *Ladies Art Catalog* in the late 1890s and was chosen as a signature or label block for this project. See details below for creating a label or signature block.

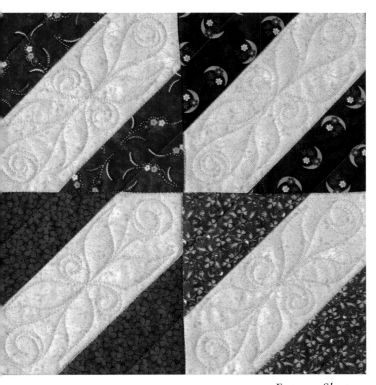

ROTARY CUTTING FOR 6" BLOCK

LIGHT BACKGROUND
4—3 1/2" squares

DARK PRINTS FOR CORNERS
8—2 1/4" squares. Draw a diagonal line on the wrong side of squares.

ROTARY CUTTING FOR 12" BLOCK

LIGHT BACKGROUND
4—6 1/2" squares

DARK PRINTS FOR CORNERS
8—4 1/2" squares. Draw a diagonal line on the wrong side of the squares.

Frances Shearer

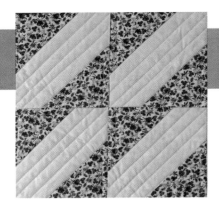
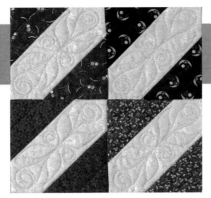

L: Betty Peister
R: Frances Shearer

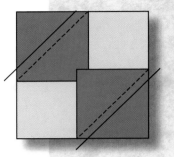

■ Lay 2 dark corner squares on a background square, right sides together. Stitch on the drawn line. Trim the seam to ¹/4" as diagrammed. Press toward the corners. Repeat three times to make a total of 4 units.

■ Assemble the block as diagrammed. Press the top row to the right and the bottom row to the left, then open the back center intersection seam as shown.

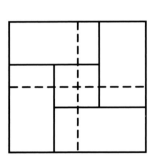

TIP
Remove 2 to 3 stitches in the seam intersection at the center of the back of the block to make it lay flat.

COLOR VARIANTS

■ If you wish to use this as a label or signature block, here are some recommendations for marking it:

❏ Determine if your block will be set on point or straight in the finished quilt. Stabilize the area to be marked by pressing freezer paper to the back of the block.

❏ If using a permanent pen, TEST it on a small piece of the fabric to make sure it does not bleed. You may also use embroidery.

❏ Heat-set the block by pressing it with a hot iron on the wrong side and the right side—be sure to use a pressing cloth so the iron does not directly touch the pen marks.

❏ Information to include: your name, quilt title, date, location

Gwen Rankin

LABELS & SIGNATURE BLOCKS

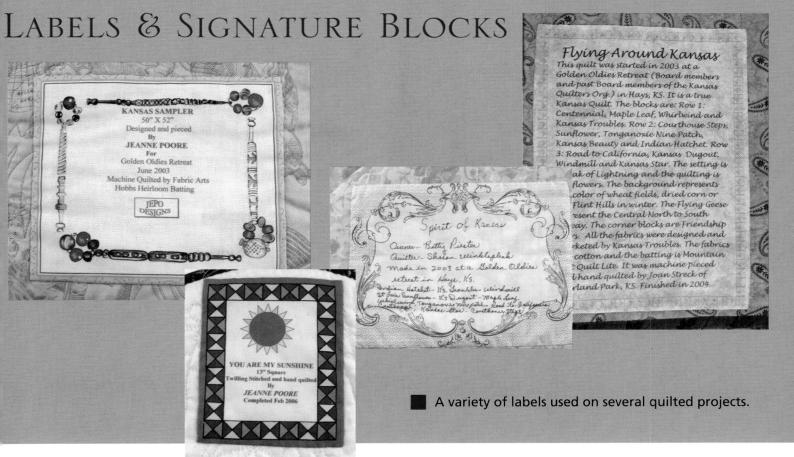

■ A variety of labels used on several quilted projects.

GALLERY   KANSAS SPIRIT   Pieced by Nadine L. Mehl-Martinitz • Quilted by Kathryn Perney

ROAD TO CALIFORNIA

Pioneers and traders traveling overland to destinations in the southwest and west passed through Kansas on the Overland, St. Joseph-California, Pike's Peak-California, Oregon, Santa Fe and Chisholm trails. Traveling by covered wagon or stagecoach or on horseback was a long, hard and dangerous trip for settlers. The trails also became major commercial highways for the delivery of goods. Wagons often were pulled by teams of oxen, with a bullwhacker walking alongside to manage and motivate them. Oxen were used because they managed better in sand and mud than mules, and it was said that Indians did not like to eat oxen. Many museums, historic markers and sites are dedicated to the trials and triumphs of the settlers on the trails. *(See the similar block Road to the White House, on page 65.)*

Joan Streck

ROTARY CUTTING FOR 6" BLOCK

LIGHT BACKGROUND
2—2 7/8" squares. Draw diagonal line on wrong side of squares.

GREEN
2—2 7/8" squares

GOLD
1—1 1/2" x 15" rectangle

RED
1—1 1/2" x 15" rectangle

ROTARY CUTTING FOR 12" BLOCK

LIGHT BACKGROUND
2—4 7/8" squares. Draw diagonal line on wrong side of squares

GREEN
2—4 7/8" squares

GOLD
1—2 1/2" x 25" rectangle

RED
1—2 1/2" x 25" rectangle

L: Joan Streck
R: Gwen Rankin

■ Place the light background square on which you drew the diagonal line onto a green square, right sides together. Stitch ¼"on both sides of the drawn line. Cut on the drawn line. Press toward the green. Repeat with the remaining background square and green square. You will get 4 half-square triangle units.

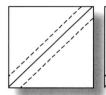  

■ Stitch the gold rectangle to the red rectangle, right sides together, along the length of the rectangles. Press toward the red rectangle. Subcut into 10—1 ½" units for the 6-inch block or 10—2 ½" units for the 12-inch block.

 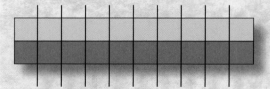

■ Stitch the light/red strip units into five 4-patch squares.

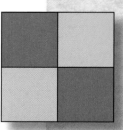

■ Stitch together in rows as diagrammed.
Press the top, bottom and center rows toward
the half-square triangle units. Then press the
rows away from the center.

COLOR VARIANTS

TONGANOXIE 9-PATCH

The town of Tonganoxie was named after the last lineal chief of the Delaware Indians. His lodge and tavern, which stood north and east of the present community, served as a stagecoach stop and trading post. By 1845 stagecoaches made regular runs from Fort Leavenworth to Fort Scott through Lawrence, stopping at the chief's lodge to pick up and deliver mail and passengers.

Carrie Hall, who lived in Leavenworth and co-wrote the 1935 book *The Romance of the Patchwork Quilt in America* with Rose Kretsinger, was invited to address the Ladies' Association of the Congregational Church in Tonganoxie. She said that the watermark on the stationery of the invitation was the inspiration for this block, noting: "There were so many roads by which you can go and come from this popular little city."

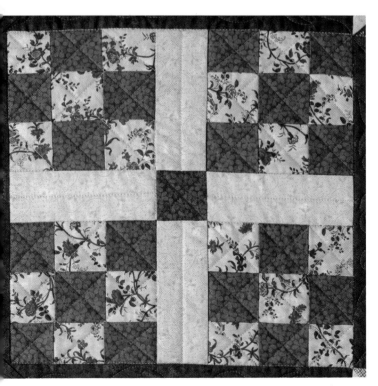

Frances Shearer

ROTARY CUTTING FOR 6" BLOCK

LIGHT BACKGROUND
1—1 3/8" x 11" rectangle
2—1 3/8" x 5 1/2" rectangles

BLUE
2—1 3/8" x 11" rectangles
1—1 3/8" x 5 1/2" rectangle
1—1 3/8" square

GOLD
4—1 3/8" x 3 1/8" rectangle

ROTARY CUTTING FOR 12" BLOCK

LIGHT BACKGROUND
1—2 1/4" x 18" rectangle
2—2 1/4" x 9" rectangles

BLUE
2—2 1/4" x 18" rectangles
1—2 1/4" x 9" rectangle
1—2 1/4" square

GOLD
4—2 1/4" x 5 3/4" rectangles

L: Frances Shearer
R: Linda K. Headings

■ Stitch the 2 short background rectangles to the top and bottom of the short blue rectangle. Press toward the blue rectangle. Subcut into 4—1 3/8" units for the 6" block and 4—2 1/4" units for the 12" block as diagrammed.

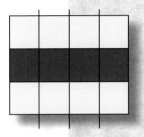

■ Stitch the 2 long blue rectangles to the top and the bottom of the long background rectangle. Press toward the blue rectangles. Subcut into 8—1 3/8" units for 6" block and 8—2 1/4" units for 12" as diagrammed.

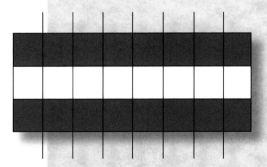

■ Assemble the units into four 9-patch blocks. Press the top, bottom and center row toward the blue fabric.

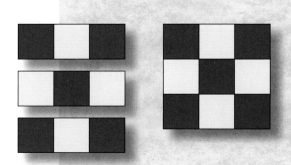

■ Stitch two 9-patch blocks to opposite sides of a gold rectangle. Repeat to make a total of 2 units—the top and bottom row. Press toward the gold rectangle.

Stitch the remaining gold rectangles to opposite sides of the blue square. Press toward the gold rectangles. Assemble the block in rows as diagrammed.

Note: You may need to trim the outside edges of these blocks to make them square at 6 1/2" and 12 1/2".

COLOR VARIANTS

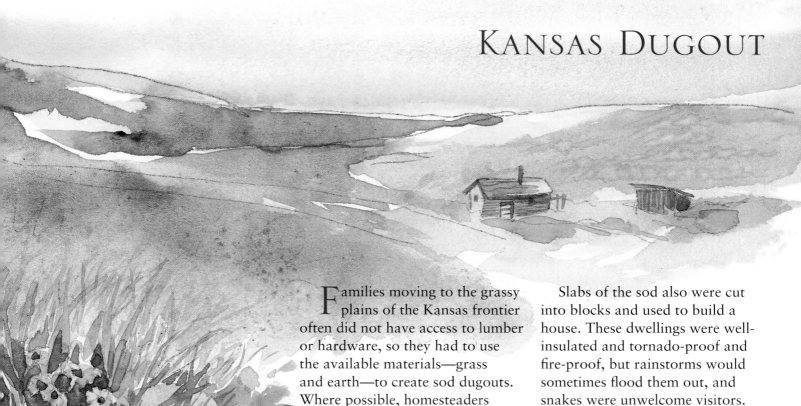

KANSAS DUGOUT

Families moving to the grassy plains of the Kansas frontier often did not have access to lumber or hardware, so they had to use the available materials—grass and earth—to create sod dugouts. Where possible, homesteaders could burrow into hillsides, leaving a hole in the roof to admit air and light. They could enlarge these dugouts with "bricks" made from buffalo grass, a short, tough native perennial whose densely tangled roots held their shape when cut.

Slabs of the sod also were cut into blocks and used to build a house. These dwellings were well-insulated and tornado-proof and fire-proof, but rainstorms would sometimes flood them out, and snakes were unwelcome visitors.

As Mark Twain noted in his 1872 book *Roughing It*: "It was the first time we had ever seen a man's front yard on top of his house."

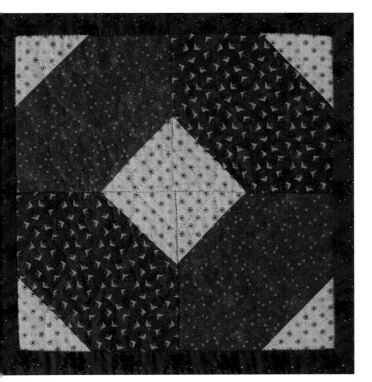

Joan Streck

ROTARY CUTTING FOR 6" BLOCK

TAN
8—1 3/4" squares. Draw a diagonal line on the wrong side of these squares.

GREEN PRINT
2—3 1/2" squares

RED PRINT
2—3 1/2" squares

ROTARY CUTTING FOR 12" BLOCK

TAN
8—3 1/4" squares. Draw a diagonal line on the wrong side of these squares.

GREEN PRINT
2—6 1/2" squares

RED PRINT
2—6 1/2" squares

L: *Jeanne Poore*
R: *Joan Streck*

■ Place 2 tan squares right sides together on opposite corners of a red square. Stitch on the line, trim to a ¼" seam allowance. Press toward the corners. Repeat this procedure to get 2 red/tan combination. Trim.

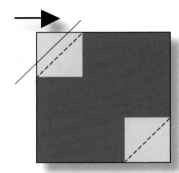 

■ Place 2 tan squares right sides together on opposite corners of a green square. Stitch on the line, trim to ¼" seam allowance. Press toward the corners. Repeat this procedure to get 2 green/tan combination.

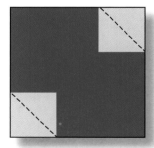 

■ Stitch the 4 units together as diagrammed.

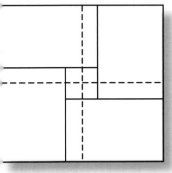

TIP
Remove 2 to 3 stitches in the seam intersection at the center of the back of the block to make it lay flat.

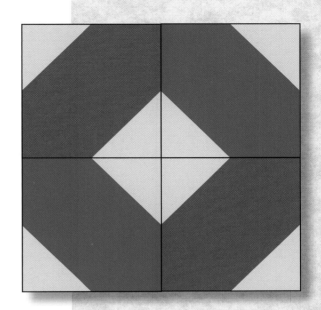

COLOR VARIANTS

WINDMILL

The windmill was used throughout the Midwest to provide water for pioneers and their animals, and as early as the 1870s these structures dotted the prairies of Kansas. Windmills, often the first visible signs of humans on the frontier, made it possible for them to secure fresh water and to establish farms and ranches in a harsh environment. The windmill was indispensable not only in pioneer times but again during the dust storms that ravished the plains states in the 1930s.

Leanna Mohr

ROTARY CUTTING FOR 6" BLOCK

LIGHT BACKGROUND
4—2" x 3 1/2" rectangles
2—2 3/8" squares. Draw a diagonal line on wrong side of squares.

GREEN
4—2 3/8" squares

GOLD
2—2 3/8" squares. Draw a diagonal line on wrong side of squares.

ROTARY CUTTING FOR 12" BLOCK

LIGHT BACKGROUND
4—3 1/2" x 6 1/2" rectangles
2—3 7/8" squares. Draw a diagonal line on wrong side of squares

GREEN
4—3 7/8" squares

GOLD
2—3 7/8" squares. Draw a diagonal line on wrong side of squares

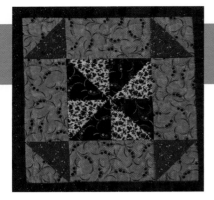 

L: Joan Streck
R: Leanna Mohr

■ Place 1 light background square onto 1 green square, right sides together. Stitch a 1/4" seam allowance on both sides of the drawn line. Cut on the drawn line. Press toward the green. Repeat to get a total of 4 background/green half-square triangle units for the corners of the block.

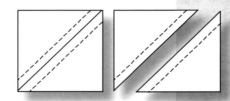 

■ Place 1 gold square onto 1 green square, right sides together. Stitch a 1/4" seam allowance on both sides of the drawn line. Cut on the drawn line. Press toward the green. Repeat to get 4 half-square triangle units for the center of the block.

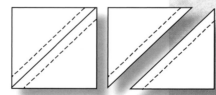 

■ Stitch the 4 gold/green half-square triangle units together as diagrammed for the center.

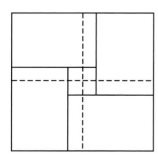

TIP
Remove 2 to 3 stitches in the seam intersection at the center of the back of the block to make it lay flat.

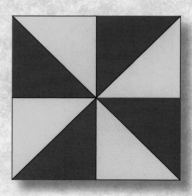

■ Stitch 1 light background rectangle to each side of the center. Press toward the rectangles.

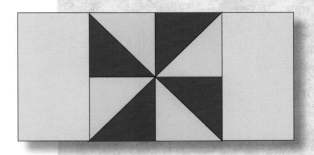

■ Stitch 1 light background/green half-square triangle unit to each side of a light background rectangle. Repeat, making sure the triangles are turning the right direction.
Press toward the rectangles.

■ Stitch the top and bottom rows to the center row of the block. Press toward the top and bottom rows.

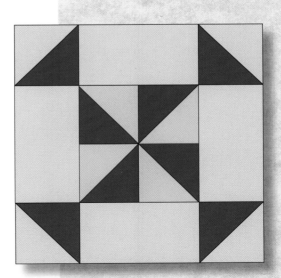

CORN & BEANS

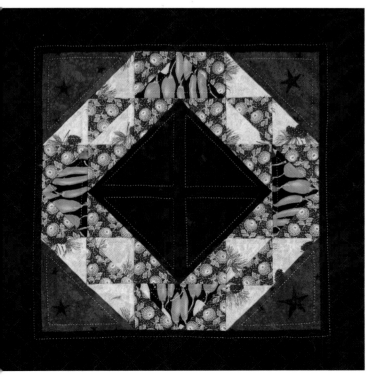

Corn & Beans—also known as Duck and Duckling, Handy Andy, Hen & Chickens and Shoofly—is an apt block to represent Kansas. The state has always been known for its crop farming. At the 1885 World's Fair in New Orleans, Kansas was awarded 65 first and second premiums, including firsts for white corn and for yellow corn and a gold medal for the best corn in the world. Today it is the nation's top wheat-growing state and ranks second in cattle brought to market. Perhaps you've seen this sign when traveling the state's highways: "One Kansas farmer feeds 129 people—plus you."

ROTARY CUTTING FOR 6" BLOCK

TAN BACKGROUND

2—2 $^7/8$" squares, subcut diagonally to get 4 triangles for outside corners

4—1 $^7/8$" squares, subcut diagonally to get 8 small triangles

6—1 $^7/8$" squares. Draw a diagonal line on the wrong side of the fabric

GREEN CENTER AND TRIANGLES

1—2 $^7/8$" square, subcut diagonally to get 2 triangles

4—1 $^7/8$" squares, subcut diagonally to get 8 triangles

2—1 $^7/8$" squares for half-square triangles

GOLD FOR CENTER

1—2 $^7/8$" square, subcut diagonally once to get 2 triangles

RED FOR FLYING GEESE

1—3 $^1/4$" square

ROTARY CUTTING FOR 12" BLOCK

TAN BACKGROUND

2—4 $^7/8$" squares, subcut diagonally to get 4 triangles for outside corners

4—2 $^7/8$" squares, subcut diagonally to get 8 small triangles

6—2 $^7/8$" squares. Draw a diagonal line on the wrong side of the fabric

GREEN CENTER AND TRIANGLES

1—4 $^7/8$" square, subcut diagonally to get 2 triangles

4—2 $^7/8$" squares, subcut each diagonally to get 8 triangles

2—2 $^7/8$" squares for half-square triangles

GOLD FOR CENTER

1—4 $^7/8$" square, subcut diagonally once to get 2 triangles

RED FOR FLYING GEESE

1—5 $^1/4$" square

Tony Muñoz

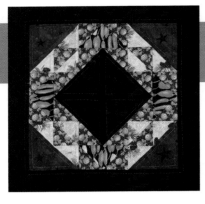

L: Tony Muñoz
R: Jeanne Poore

■ Align 2 small tan squares on which you drew the diagonal lines on the 2 green squares, right sides together. Stitch 1/4" on both sides of the drawn line. Cut on drawn line. Press toward the green. You will get 4 half-square triangle units.

Stitch 2 small tan triangles to adjacent sides of a half-square triangle unit as diagrammed (1). Press toward the tan triangles. Repeat to make 4 pieced units.

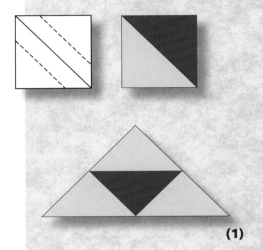

(1)

■ Stitch 2 of unit #1 to 2 large green triangles and 2 of unit #1 to the 2 large gold triangles as diagrammed (2), matching the center of the long edge of the large triangle to the intersecting seam of the small tan triangles. Press toward the large triangles.

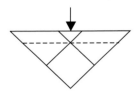

TIP
Stitch the pieced unit on top of the large triangle to make sure you get a sharp point. Make sure your stitches are inside the V where the small triangles intersect.

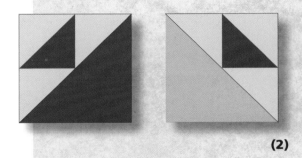

(2)

■ Stitch the 4 units together to make the center of the block as diagrammed (3).

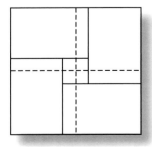

TIP
Remove 2 to 3 stitches in the seam intersection at the center of the back of the block to make it lay flat.

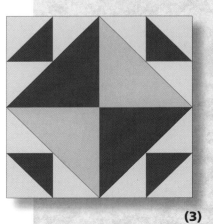

(3)

40 ◁◁◁◁- - - - - - - - - - - - - - - - -

■ Align 2 tan squares on which you drew the diagonal line on opposite corners of the red square. Stitch a 1/4" seam allowance on both sides of the drawn line (4). The squares do overlap in the center. Cut on the drawn line (5). Press toward the tan triangles (6)

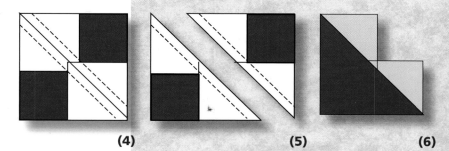

(4) **(5)** **(6)**

■ Place another tan square on the corner of the red triangle as diagrammed (7). Stitch a 1/4" seam allowance on both sides of the drawn line. Cut on the line. Press toward the tan triangles. Repeat for the remaining unit. You will have 4 flying geese units.

(7)

■ Stitch 2 green triangles on opposite ends of the flying geese units as diagrammed (8). Press toward the green triangles. Repeat to make 4 units.

(8)

■ Stitch a unit (8) to opposite sides of the center of the block. Press toward the flying geese unit. Stitch the remaining 2 flying geese units (8) to the opposite sides. Press toward the flying geese units.

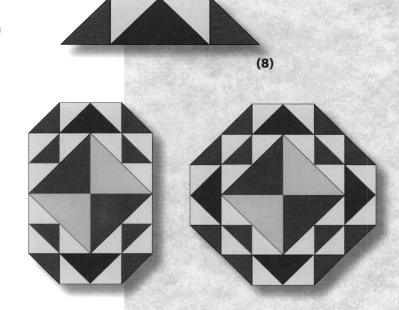

Stitch the 4 large tan triangles to the four corners. Press toward the corners.

KANSAS TROUBLES

Kansas Troubles is a very old pattern associated with the border wars between Kansas and Missouri settlers before and during the Civil War. Traditionally the block is made with red in it to represent "Bleeding Kansas," as the tumultuous state was called in its territorial days. There are records of the pattern being published in periodicals as far back as the 1890s, but we do not know if this pattern actually existed during the Civil War. However, it does symbolize the many challenges and difficulties settlers encountered while making their homes in Kansas.

Nadine L. Mehl-Martinitz

ROTARY CUTTING FOR 6" BLOCK

LIGHT BACKGROUND

2—3 $7/8$" squares. Subcut each once diagonally to get 4 triangles.

8—1 $5/8$" squares. Draw a diagonal line on the wrong side of each square.

4—1 $1/4$" squares

BLACK FOR MEDIUM TRIANGLES

2—2 $3/8$" squares. Subcut each once diagonally to get 4 triangles.

RED FOR POINTS

12—1 $5/8$" squares. Subcut *only* 4 of the squares once diagonally, to get 8 small triangles.

ROTARY CUTTING FOR 12" BLOCK

LIGHT BACKGROUND

2—6 $7/8$" squares. Subcut each once diagonally to get 4 large triangles.

8—2 $3/8$" squares. Draw a diagonal line on the wrong side of each square.

4—2" squares

BLACK FOR MEDIUM TRIANGLES

2—3 $7/8$" squares. Subcut each once diagonally to get 4 medium triangles.

RED FOR CENTERS AND CORNERS

12—2 $3/8$" squares, subcut *only* 4 of the squares once diagonally to get 8 small triangles.

L: Nadine L. Mehl-Martinitz
R: Jeanne Poore

■ Place the 8 light background squares on the 8 dark squares, right sides together. Stitch 1/4" on both sides of the drawn line. Cut on drawn line. Press toward the dark fabric. You will get 16 half-square triangle units.

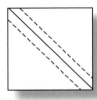 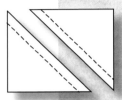 

■ Stitch 4 units together as diagrammed below (Unit A), using two of the triangle units and one of the small red triangles. Press toward the single red triangle.

Unit A

■ Stitch 4 units together as diagrammed in Unit B, adding the small background square. Press toward the square.
Note: Stitch exactly as diagrammed.

Unit B

■ Stitch Unit A to the top edge of the medium triangle. Press toward the medium triangle. Stitch Unit B to the side of the medium triangle/Unit A segment. Press toward the medium triangle.

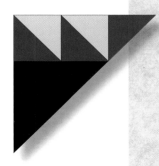
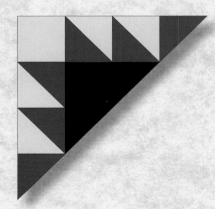

■ Stitch the large background triangles to the pieced units, being careful to match the center of the long edge of the large triangle to the center of the pieced units. Pin at the center and both ends. Stitch with the pieced unit on top. Press toward the large triangle.

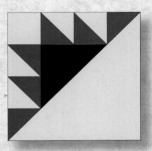

■ Assemble into the block as diagrammed below.

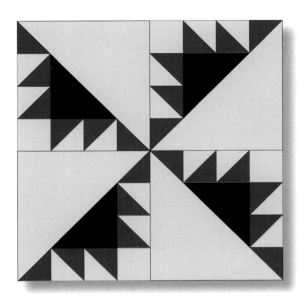

TIP
Remove 2 to 3 stitches in the seam intersection at the center of the back of the block to make it lay flat.

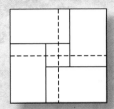

GALLERY   SPIRIT OF KANSAS   Pieced by Betty Piester • Quilted by Sharon Winklepleck

KANSAS STAR

Kansas was admitted to the Union Jan. 29, 1861, as the 34th state. Its flag bears 34 stars and the Latin motto *Ad Astra Per Aspera*: "To the Stars Through Difficulties," acknowledging the chaos, battles and political infighting that dominated life between the opening of the territory in May 1854 and statehood almost seven years later. The anti-slavery forces ultimately won, and Kansas was a free state. A state senator, John James Ingalls of Atchison, designed the state seal, featured on the flag, and created the motto. Less than three months after Kansas became a state, the Civil War began.

ROTARY CUTTING FOR 6" BLOCK

LIGHT BACKGROUND
10—1 $7/8$" squares. Subcut each once diagonally to get 20 triangles.
4—2" squares

RED FOR STAR POINTS
4—1 $7/8$" squares. Subcut each once diagonally to get 8 triangles.

DARK GREEN SQUARES
5—2" squares

DARK FOR OUTER EDGE TRIANGLES
4—1 $7/8$" squares. Subcut each once diagonally to get 8 triangles.

ROTARY CUTTING FOR 12" BLOCK

LIGHT BACKGROUND
10—2 $7/8$" squares. Subcut each once diagonally to get 20 triangles.
4—3 $3/8$" squares

RED FOR STAR POINTS
4—2 $7/8$" squares. Subcut each once diagonally to get 8 triangles.

DARK GREEN SQUARES
5—3 $3/8$" squares

DARK FOR OUTER EDGE TRIANGLES
4—2 $7/8$" squares. Subcut each once diagonally to get 8 triangles.

Joan Streck

L: Joan Streck
R: Jeanne Poore

■ Stitch 2 background triangles to opposite sides of a dark green square, matching the center of the long edge of the triangle to the center of the edge of the square as diagrammed. Press toward the background triangles.

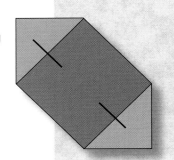

■ Stitch 2 more triangles to the other sides of the square, again matching the center of the edges. Press toward the triangles. Repeat to make 5 of these units.

■ Stitch 1 red triangle and 1 dark triangle to opposite sides of the light background square, matching the centers of the sides as diagrammed. Press toward the triangles.

Stitch another red triangle and dark triangle to the remaining opposite sides. Press toward the triangles. Repeat to make 4 of these units.

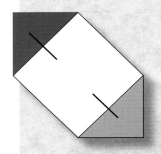
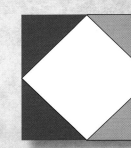

■ Stitch units together in rows as shown. I suggest you press the top and bottom rows toward the center square and the center row away from the center square. However, you may wish to press all the joining seams open.

COURTHOUSE STEPS

CHASE COUNTY
COURTHOUSE IN
COTTONWOOD FALLS

In many towns in Kansas and across the country, the county courthouse was the site of much activity. Important property, tax and legal records were kept there; county and civic officials and lawyers often had their offices there, and jails were even built in some courthouses. The Chase County Courthouse in Cottonwood Falls, built in 1873 of native limestone and designed in the French Renaissance style, is the oldest operating courthouse in the state-—and one of the most distinctive.

The Courthouse Steps quilt block is a variation of the Log Cabin design dating to the mid-1800s in America. The name "Log Cabin" is thought to be associated with the 1859-60 presidential campaign of Abraham Lincoln, and the pattern proved very popular before and after the Civil War.

ROTARY CUTTING FOR 6" BLOCK

LIGHT LOGS
2—1¼" x 2" rectangles
2—1¼" x 3½" rectangles
2—1¼" x 5" rectangles

DARK LOGS
2—1¼" x 3½" rectangles
2—1¼" x 5" rectangles
2—1¼" x 6½" rectangles

RED CENTER
1—2" square

ROTARY CUTTING FOR 12" BLOCK

LIGHT LOGS
2—2" x 3½" rectangles
2—2" x 6½" rectangles
2—2" x 9½" rectangles

DARK LOGS
2—2" x 6½" rectangles
2—2" x 9½" rectangles
2—2" x 12½" rectangles

RED CENTERS
1—3½" square

Betty Piester reversed light and dark fabrics on this block.

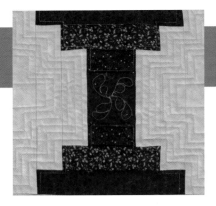

L: Betty Piester
R: Nancy Austin Swanwick

■ Stitch the two shortest light logs on opposite sides of the center square. All seams are pressed away from the center square, toward the logs, in each piecing step.

■ Stitch the two shortest dark logs on opposite sides of the pieced unit. I recommend you carefully measure the blocks after each complete round to make sure the block is square.

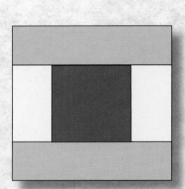

■ Continue around the block, alternating the light logs and dark logs until you have 3 logs on all sides.

KANSAS SPIRIT   Nadine L. Mehl-Martinitz

GALLERY   PIONEER SPIRIT   Pieced by Pam Calhoun • Quilted by Beth Cronhardt

WHIRLWIND

No book of quilt patterns relating to Kansas would be complete without the Whirlwind block. And certainly the movie "The Wizard of Oz" made tornadoes synonymous with our state.

Golden Oldie quilter Jeannine Bryan's husband was caught in a tornado and survived without a scratch, even though the hay barn he was near was destroyed. Jeanne Poore's grandparents' farm home and barn were destroyed by a tornado July 4, 1932, in Washington County near Morrowville.

Only one small section of the kitchen wall, the smokehouse and the Model A Ford that was tossed into a field survived. But the family rebuilt the farm and persevered, as countless others have done for generations.

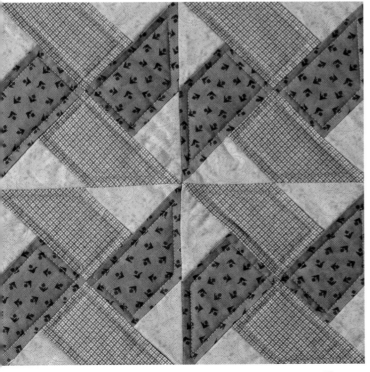

Frances Shearer

ROTARY CUTTING FOR 6" BLOCK

LIGHT BACKGROUND
4—2 ³/4" squares. Subcut each diagonally twice to get a total of 16 triangles.

GREEN PRINT
4—1 ¹/2" x 4 ¹/2" rectangles. Subcut each in half at a 45-degree angle to get 8 trapezoids that measure 1 ¹/2" x 3". Cut all fabric with the right side up.

GOLD PRINT
4—1 ¹/2" x 4 ¹/2" rectangles. Subcut each in half at a 45-degree angle to get 8 trapezoids that measure 1 ¹/2" x 3". Cut all fabric with the right side up.

ROTARY CUTTING FOR 12" BLOCK

LIGHT BACKGROUND
4—4 ¹/4" squares. Subcut each diagonally twice to get a total of 16 triangles.

GREEN PRINT
4—2 ⁵/8" x 7 ⁵/8" rectangles. Subcut each in half at a 45-degree angle to get 8 trapezoids that measure 2 ⁵/8" x 5 ¹/8". Cut all fabric with the right side up.

GOLD PRINT
4—2 ⁵/8" x 7 ⁵/8" rectangles. Subcut each in half at a 45-degree angle to get 8 trapezoids that measure 2 ⁵/8" x 5 ¹/8". Cut all fabric with the right side up.

 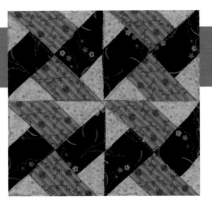

L: Frances Shearer
R: Nadine L. Mehl-Martinitz

■ Stitch a green trapezoid onto a small background triangle as diagrammed. Press toward the dark trapezoid. (By stitching the trapezoid onto the triangle you will be stitching from a straight edge.) Repeat to make 8 units. The 45-degree angle on the green is a bias edge. Be careful when pressing so you do not stretch the bias.

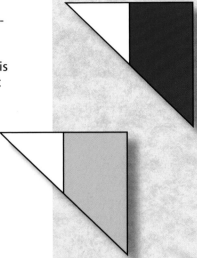

Stitch a gold trapezoid onto a small background triangle as diagrammed. Repeat as above to make 8 units.

■ Stitch a gold/background unit to a green/background unit. Press toward the green/background unit. Make 8 of these units.

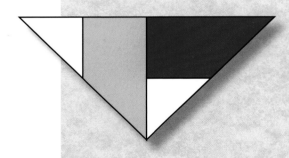

■ Stitch 2 of these units together. Make 4 of these units.

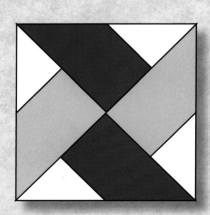

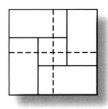

TIP
Remove the 2 to 3 stitches in the seam intersection at the center of the back of the block to make it lay flat.

■ Assemble block as diagrammed. Press the top row
to the right and the bottom row to the left. Again,
open the center back seam to make the block lay flat.

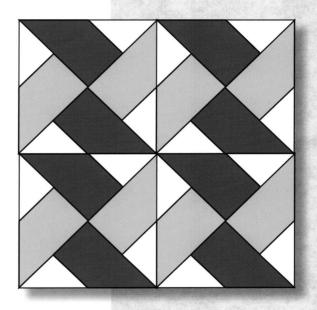

COLOR VARIANTS

SPIRIT OF KANSAS   Betty Pieste

FLINT HILLS

Quilter Joan Streck selected this block because it is one of her favorites.

She says, "If you take the time to really look at the scenery in all the seasons, Kansas is a beautiful state."

One of the state's nicknames is "Garden of the West," because of the beauty of the landscape and the fertility of the soil. Some historians think the nickname may have been promoted by Northern newspapers in an attempt to encourage people to settle in the territory to counteract the followers of the pro-slavery movement populating it in the years leading up to statehood.

Kansas has other nicknames: "The Sunflower State," "The Wheat State," "Midway, USA," "The Central State," "The Jayhawk State," "Bleeding Kansas," "Squatter State" and "The Battleground of Freedom."

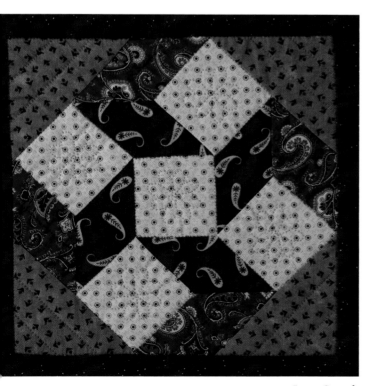

Joan Streck

TEMPLATES
6" PATTERN

A—Cut 4 gold for outer corners

B—Cut 4 red diamonds

C—Cut 4 light squares

D—Cut 4 green diamonds

E—Cut 1 light square

12" PATTERN

A—Cut 4 gold for outer corners

B—Cut 4 red diamonds

C—Cut 4 light squares

D—Cut 4 green diamonds

E—Cut 1 light square

L: Joan Streck
R: Jeanne Poore

■ Carefully mark with a dot the ¹/4″ seam allowance at the corners of the diamond and square pieces.

Stitch a red B diamond to a green D diamond, starting at the ¹/4″ seam-allowance dot at the inner corners. Make 4 of these units. Do not press at this time.

■ Carefully pin the light C square, right sides together, to the green diamond, matching the ¹/4″ seam-allowance dot and starting and stopping at the dot. Pin the adjacent side of the square to the red diamond and stitch from the ¹/4″ seam-allowance dot to the edge. Press the seam allowances open. Repeat to make 4 units.

■ Stitch the green diamond edge to the center E square, starting and stopping at the ¹/4″ seam-allowance dot.

■ Stitch another unit with the green diamond edge to the center E square, starting and stopping at the ¹/4″ seam-allowance dot. Now join the seam between the green diamond and the light C square, starting at the center and stitching to the outside edge. Press the seam open.

■ Continue around the center E square until all 4 units have been stitched.

Mark the center of the long diagonal edge of the 4 gold A triangles.

■ Stitch a gold A triangle to the center unit, matching the mark with the seam between the light square and red diamond. Press toward the triangle. Repeat around the block.

60 ◁◁◁◁ –

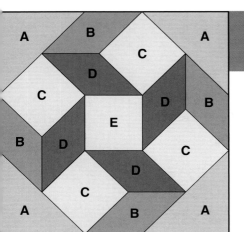

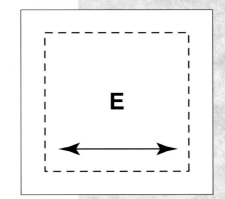

E

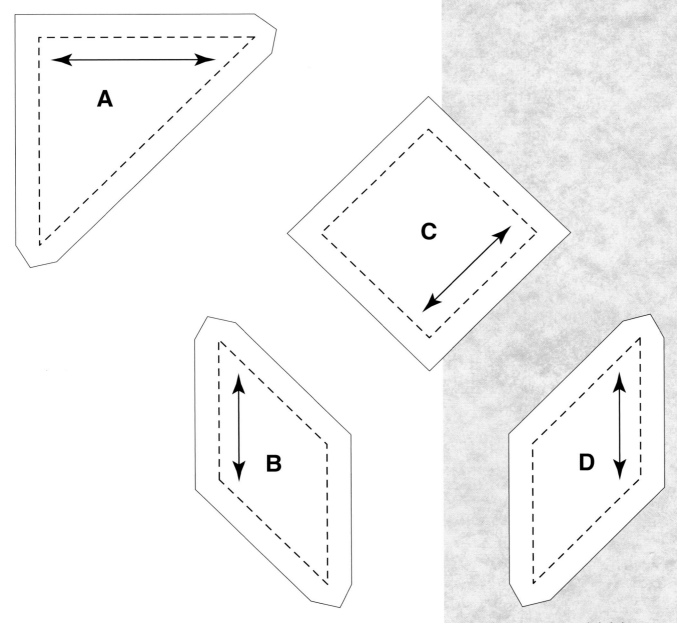

A

C

B

D

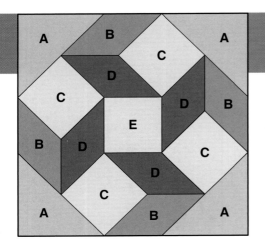

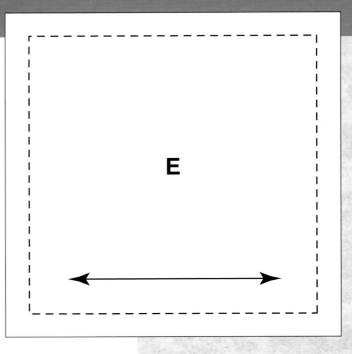

E

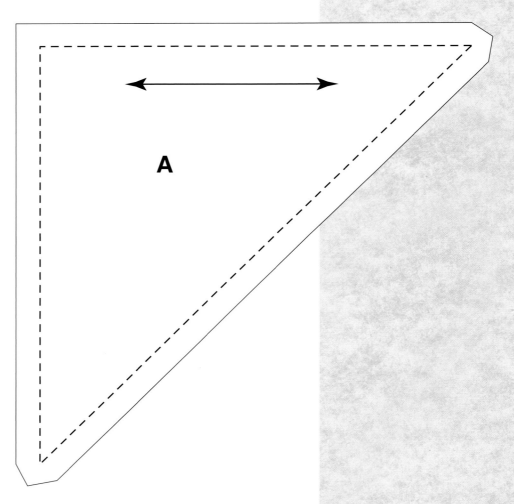

A

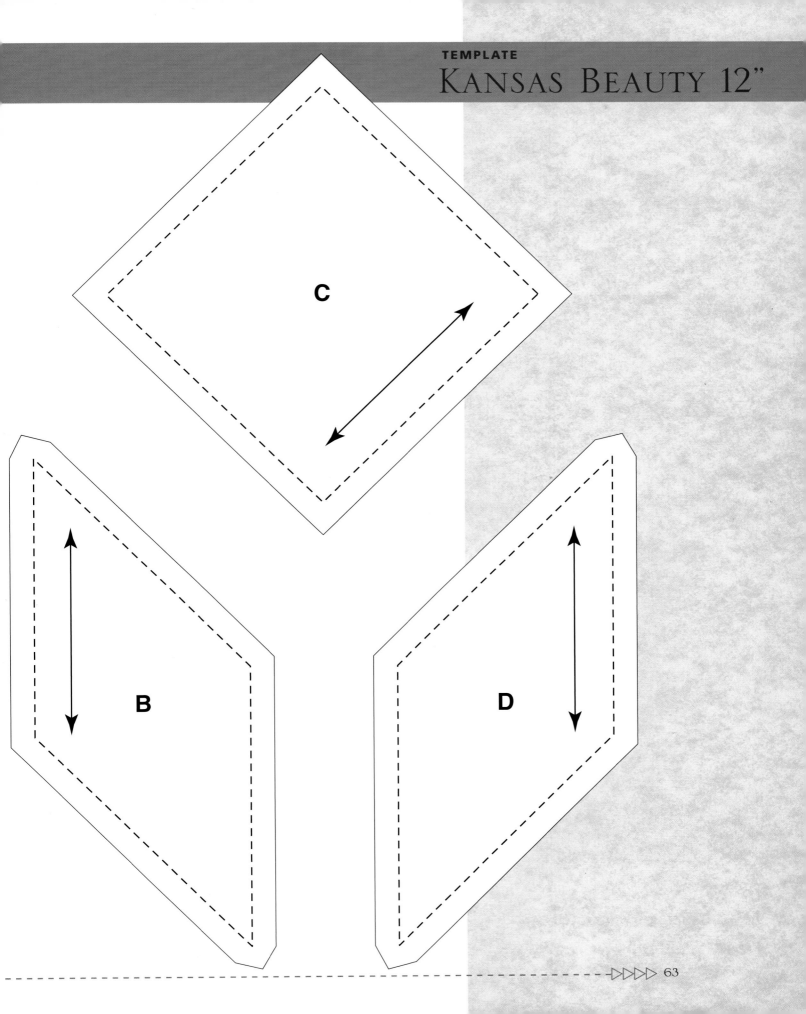

C

B

D

GALLERY   KANSAS SAMPLER   Pieced and quilted by LaRue Nues

ROAD TO THE WHITE HOUSE

The 34th president of the United States, Dwight D. Eisenhower (1890-1969), grew up in Abilene. After stellar service as supreme commander of the Allied forces in World War II, he was named supreme commander of the new NATO armed forces. He was persuaded to run for president in 1952 as a Republican, and his engaging grin perfectly complemented his campaign slogan: "I Like Ike." He was re-elected in 1956.

Two other native sons were candidates for the White House: Topekan Alf Landon, governor of Kansas from 1933 to 1937, made an unsuccessful bid in 1936,

running against incumbent Franklin D. Roosevelt. (Landon's daughter, Nancy Landon Kassebaum Baker, represented Kansas in the U.S. Senate from 1978 to 1997.) Bob Dole of Russell, a member of the U.S. Senate from 1968 to 1996, was the Republican candidate for vice president in 1976 and for president in 1996, losing the election to incumbent Bill Clinton.

This block is very similar to the Road to California block on page 23.

ROTARY CUTTING FOR 6" BLOCK

LIGHT BACKGROUND

2—2 1/2" squares

1—1 $^1/_2$" x 9" rectangle

RED

2—2 $^7/_8$" squares. Draw a diagonal line on wrong side of squares.

1—1 $^1/_2$" x 9" rectangle

BLACK

2—2 $^7/_8$" squares

ROTARY CUTTING FOR 12" BLOCK

LIGHT BACKGROUND

2—4 1/2" squares

1—2 $^1/_2$" x 15" rectangle

RED

2—4 $^7/_8$" squares. Draw a diagonal line on wrong side of squares.

1—2 $^1/_2$" x 15" rectangle

BLACK

2—4 $^7/_8$" squares

Jeanne Poore

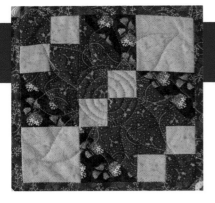

L: Jeanne Poore
R: Frances Shearer

■ Place a red square onto a black square, right sides together. Stitch ¼" on both sides of the drawn line. Cut on the drawn line. Press toward the black. Repeat with the remaining red square and black square. You will get 4 half-square triangle units.

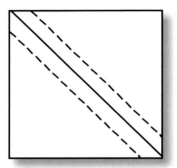
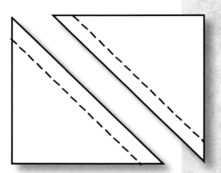

■ Right sides together, stitch the light background rectangle to the red rectangle along the length. Press toward the red rectangle. Subcut into 6—1 ½" units for the 6-inch block or 6—2 ½" units for the 12-inch block. You will get a total of 6 units

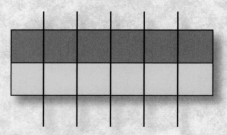

■ Stitch the light/red strip units into three 4-patch squares.

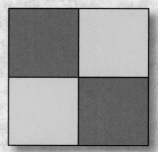

■ Stitch together in rows as diagrammed. Press the top and bottom rows away from the half-square triangle unit and the center row toward the 4-patch. Then press the rows away from the center.

MAPLE LEAF

Maple trees in all their varieties are among North America's sturdiest, most versatile and most beloved deciduous trees. In the fall the leaves turn brilliant shades of red, yellow and orange, a colorful spectacle celebrated since 1957 at the annual Maple Leaf Festival in Baldwin City the third weekend in October. Maple wood is excellent for making beautiful fine-grained furniture and as a source of fuel that can be made into high-quality charcoal. The sap of maple trees also can be made into sugar and syrup.

Jeanne Poore

ROTARY CUTTING FOR 6" BLOCK

LIGHT BACKGROUND
2—2 7/8" squares. Draw a diagonal line on the wrong side of the squares.
2—2 1/2" squares

RED FOR CENTERS
3—2 1/2" squares
2—2 7/8" squares
1—3 1/4" x 1" rectangle

ROTARY CUTTING FOR 12" BLOCK

LIGHT BACKGROUND
2—4 7/8" squares. Draw a diagonal line on the wrong side of the squares.
2—4 1/2" squares

RED FOR CENTERS AND CORNERS
3—4 1/2" squares
2—4 7/8" squares
1—2" x 7" rectangle

L: Jeanne Poore
R: Frances Shearer

■ Turn under and press a ¼" seam allowance for the rectangle strip. Center the strip on the diagonal of one of the background squares. The strip will be slightly longer than the diagonal of the square. Stitch to square. You may choose to top-stitch with a sewing machine, use invisible machine appliqué or hand appliqué the rectangle to the square. Trim the ends to match the square.

■ Place one light background square onto one red square, right sides together. Stitch ¼" on both sides of the drawn line. Cut on the drawn line. Press toward the red. Repeat to get a total of 4 background/red half-square triangle units.

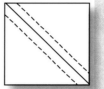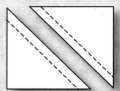

■ Arrange half-square pieced and plain squares together as diagrammed. Press top and bottom rows to the left and the center row to the right.

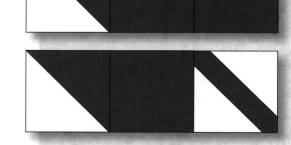

Mini Maple Leaf   Jeanne Poore

Jeanne Poore

STATE FAIR SUNFLOWER

The sunflower is the Kansas state flower, and the hardy prairie bloom is a favorite symbol. The highest point in Kansas is Mount Sunflower, elevation 4,039 feet, and the monument marking the site just a mile from the Colorado border is a towering sunflower made of railroad spikes.

The northwest Kansas town of Goodland calls itself the "Sunflower Capital of the World" and it commemorates that distinction with a 32-foot replica of one of Vincent van Gogh's sunflower paintings created by Canadian artist Cameron Cross. Bill Nicks, director of Lenexa Parks and Recreation, claims to have the world's largest collection of sunflower items—more than 2,500 pieces. All around the state are Sunflower theaters, Sunflower motels, Sunflower cafes—even a Sunflower bread company.

The Kansas State Fair, advertised as the state's largest event and featuring 280 acres of activities, is held in the south-central city of Hutchinson each September. Hutchinson is the home of the Kansas Cosmosphere and Space Center and also the site of the new Kansas Underground Salt Museum, the only museum in the Western Hemisphere housed in a working salt mine, 650 feet below the surface. One of the 300,000 boxes of films stored in the climate-controlled space there is "The Wizard of Oz."

Joan Streck

ROTARY CUTTING FOR 6" BLOCK

LIGHT BACKGROUND
12—1 1/2" squares. Draw a diagonal line on the wrong side of 8 of the squares.
4—1 1/2" x 2 1/2" rectangles

YELLOW GOLD PETALS
8—1 1/2" x 2 1/2" rectangles
4—1" squares. Draw a diagonal line on the wrong side of these squares.

GREEN LEAVES
4—1 1/2" squares

CENTER
1—2 1/2" square

ROTARY CUTTING FOR 12" BLOCK

LIGHT BACKGROUND
12—2 1/2" squares. Draw a diagonal line on the wrong side of 8 of the squares.
4—2 1/2" x 4 1/2" rectangles

YELLOW GOLD PETALS
8—2 1/2" x 4 1/2" rectangles
4—1 1/2"" squares. Draw a diagonal line on the wrong side of these squares.

GREEN LEAVES
4—2 1/2" squares

CENTER
1—4 1/2" square

L: Joan Streck
R: Betty Piester

■ Place the small petal squares, right sides together, on the corners of the center square. Stitch on the drawn lines. Trim the corners to ¼" seam allowance. Press toward the corners.

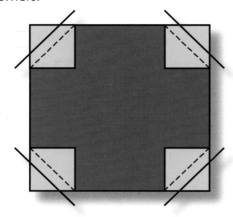
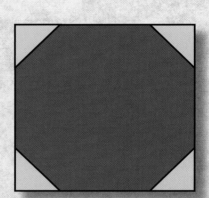

■ Stitch a light background square onto the petal rectangle on the drawn line. Be sure to stitch exactly as diagrammed. Trim to ¼" seam allowance. Press toward the light background triangle. Repeat with the remaining petal rectangles and 7 of the light background squares for a total of 8 petals.

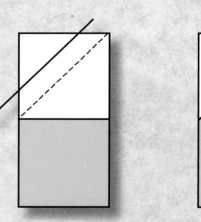

■ Stitch a light background square to a green leaf square as diagrammed. Repeat to make 4 units.

■ Stitch 2 light background rectangles to 2 of the green leaf units as diagrammed in illustration A. Stitch the 2 remaining background units to the 2 remaining units as in illustration B. Press toward the rectangles.

A 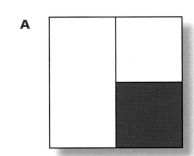   B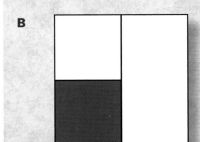

■ Assemble block in rows. Press the top and bottom rows in toward the petals and the center row out toward the petals.

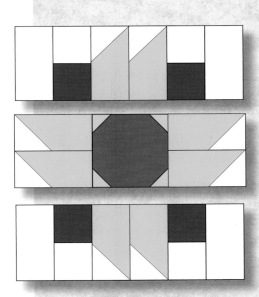

STITCHING DETAILS & COLOR VARIANTS

BASIC INSTRUCTIONS

FABRIC SELECTION

Individuals spend many hours in planning, cutting and piecing a quilt. Therefore, they should select good-quality fabrics, including the backing for the quilt.

Whether to wash the fabric is a topic that has been debated by many. Some people wash their fabric, then starch it to make it easier to cut. Washing does remove the sizing that makes fabrics look good in the stores and also gives fabric a longer shelf life. My fabric stash, which is sizable, keeps increasing, and some of it has been around for a number of years. So I no longer wash the fabric as soon as I take it home unless I know that I intend to hand quilt a project. Then I wash the fabric—and be sure to wash the quilt backing, too.

My main concerns for washing are color-fastness and shrinkage. The thread counts are not always consistent anymore, so a fabric may not shrink uniformly. I do recommend testing dark fabrics to see if they will bleed. You definitely do not want the dye to transfer to other portions of your quilt after you have completed the project.

If you do have a fabric that loses color, wash it several times if needed. If it continues to lose color, select another fabric. If you wash one fabric for a quilt, wash all of them before cutting and piecing.

ROTARY CUTTING TOOLS

Rotary cutting has brought speed and accuracy to quilt making by allowing quilters to easily cut strips of fabric and then cut those strips into small pieces.

The three tools necessary for rotary cutting are cutters, rulers and mats.

CUTTERS

Rotary cutters now come in four sizes: 18, 28, 45 and 60 millimeters in diameter. They have sharp round blades that are replaceable.

Be very careful handling these tools. Store them safely away where hildren and pets will not be able to reach them. Always close the blades after each and every step in the cutting process.

There are various brands and styles available. I prefer ergonomic cutters with curved, padded handles. Since the patterns in this book come in two sizes, you may find that the 28 mm and 45 mm sizes work best.

RULERS

Rotary rulers are made of transparent acrylic to enable the quilter to see the fabric underneath. You need rulers with clear markings in measurements of $1/8$, $1/4$, $1/2$, $3/4$ and 1 inch. A good selection of rulers should include 6 $1/2$", 9 $1/2$" and 12 $1/2$" squares and 3" x 18", 6" x 12" and 6" x 24" rectangles. Because the projects in this book include small and large squares, these sizes are recommended. Many smaller and larger sizes, as well as specialized shapes, can be very helpful on other projects.

MATS

The cutting mat provides a tough work surface that not only protects your table from the blade but also preserves the blade and makes cutting easier.

Its color should contrast with your fabrics, and the mats now come in green, gray, lavender, purple and black.

The mats are self-healing but eventually will develop surface scratches. If the grooves from the scratches become a problem while cutting, replace the mat. You may be able to cut a small section off to use next to your sewing machine or for miniature projects.

The mats come in many sizes, from as small as 6" x 8" to one that is 40" x 72" for use on a table top. I recommend the 18" x 24" for beginning quilters.

Although the mats come with a 1" grid, they are not always accurate for measuring. The lines are useful for aligning the edges to start cutting but not for measuring. Use your rulers to measure the cuts of fabric. I recommend turning the mats to the plain side to avoid the distraction of the printed lines.

Do not iron on the mats or leave them in a hot car, as they will warp. Always store the mat flat.

BASIC INSTRUCTIONS

ROTARY CUTTING

Place fabric on work surface with fold closest to you.

Cut all strips from selvage edge to selvage edge the width of the fabric unless otherwise indicated in project instructions.

Square left edge of fabric using rotary cutter and rulers.

To cut each strip required for a project, place the ruler over the cut edge of the fabric, aligning desired marking on the ruler with the edge; make cut.

TEMPLATE CUTTING

The piecing templates include ¼" seam allowance. Place the template on wrong side of fabric, aligning grain line on template with straight grain of fabric.

Use a sharp fabric marking pencil to draw around the template. Check template against original pattern for accuracy.

Cut out fabric piece using rotary cutter of sharp fabric scissors. Be sure to lay out your pieces according to the diagrams for the block pattern.

PIECING

Set sewing machine stitch length to 10 to 11 stitches per inch. Many of the newer machines have an automatic setting when it is turned on.

An accurate ¼" seam allowance is essential. Presser feet that are ¼" wide are available for most sewing machines. If you do not have an accurate presser foot, create a seam guide by placing the edge of a piece of tape, a stack of post-it notes or a magnetic seam guide ¼" from the needle.

When piecing, always place pieces right sides together and match raw edges; pin if necessary.

Chain piecing saves time and will usually result in more accurate piecing. Make a thread saver by folding a small square of fabric in half and stitching across it, leaving your presser foot down. Then feed pairs of pattern pieces through the machine. When all the pieces are sewn together, stitch across a second thread saver. This method saves thread and increases your efficiency.

When sewing across seam intersections, place pieces right sides together and match seams exactly, making sure seam allowances are pressed in opposite directions.

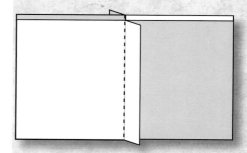

PRESSING

I prefer to use a steam iron set on Cotton for pressing. Press after sewing each seam.

Seam allowances are usually pressed to one side, usually toward the darker fabric. However, to reduce bulk it may occasionally be necessary to press seam allowances toward the lighter fabric or to press them open. Each block has pressing steps included.

To prevent a dark fabric seam allowance from showing through a light fabric, trim the darker seam allowance slightly narrower than the light seam allowance.

To press long seams, such as those in strip sets, lay strips across the width of the ironing board.

FINISHING THE QUILT

BATTING SELECTION

Batting is the layer between the quilt top and the back that provides the loft and also the warmth in a quilt. It can be made of 100 percent polyester, 100 percent cotton in several weights, or a combination of both. There are also wool and silk batts as well as new blends of these with cotton and polyester. Wool and silk batts are more expensive.

Carefully read the qualities, distance between stitching and care instructions on any batting you are selecting. Choosing the right batting will make your quilting easier. If you are machine quilting, choose a low-loft, all-cotton or cotton/polyester blend batting. If you are having a professional machine quilt your project, you should discuss batting options beforehand.

Make sure your batting is larger than the quilt top.

QUILTING

The quilts in this book have been both hand quilted and machine quilted.

HAND QUILTING

I recommended that you mark your quilt top before layering it with the batting and backing. If you are doing simple outline, echo or in-the-ditch quilting, you will not need to mark your quilt. If you are using small motifs, you can mark them as you go.

Many precut quilting stencils as well as books of quilting patterns are available from which to choose designs.

Quilting lines may be marked using fabric marking pencils, chalk markers, water- or air-soluble pens, or lead pencils. DO NOT PRESS the top after you mark it.

PROFESSIONAL MACHINE QUILTING

The quilter may have a large selection of designs or specialties that may be used on the quilt. Discuss the design elements so you both have a clear understanding of the finished project. Remember that this is your quilt and you need to be happy with the results.

Quilt Backing

Considering the time and expense of making the quilt top plus the quilting, choose the best quality of fabric for the backing.

The quilt backing should be a minimum of 4" larger than the top on all sides. If you are having your quilt professionally machine quilted, the professional may request even more. Be sure to check with the machine quilter.

Measure length and width of the quilt top and add the appropriate inches (4" or more) to each measurement.

Quilt backings come in 90", 108" and 120" sizes, or you can piece the backing with two to three strips of 45" wide fabrics. Pressing the seams open for pieced backings is recommended.

Binding

The binding encloses the raw edges of your quilt. There are two kinds of binding—bias and straight. Bias binding is used for curves or round corners and as a design element to create spirals, stripes and plaids on the edges of quilts. The bindings in the instructions for the two sizes of finished quilts in this book are straight bindings.

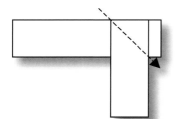

In the finished quilt instructions you are told to cut your binding strips 2" to 2 1/2". The choice is yours, depending on the finished width you desire.

Cut the number of crosswise strips of binding fabric the width of the fabric in the project instructions. Lay the fabric strips right sides together and sew in the direction shown for a 45-degree angle to make a continuous strip of the binding. Press seams open as diagrammed.

Matching wrong sides and raw edges, fold and press strip in half lengthwise.

Attaching the binding

I recommend using a walking foot to stitch the binding to your quilt.

On the front of the quilt top, put one end of your binding strip on a long side edge and lay binding around the quilt to make sure that the binding seams do not end up at a corner. Adjust placement if necessary.

Match the raw edges of the binding to the raw edges of the quilt top and pin to right side of quilt along one edge.

Starting 8" to 10" from the beginning of the binding strip, stitch 1/4" along the edge to within 1/4" of the first corner. With needle in down position, lift pressure foot and pivot quilt top. Stitch diagonally to the corner.

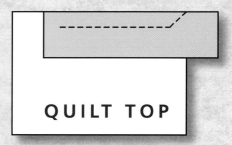

QUILT TOP

Lift needle and clip thread.

Fold binding as diagrammed, first away from quilt top, then back down along the next raw edge of the quilt.

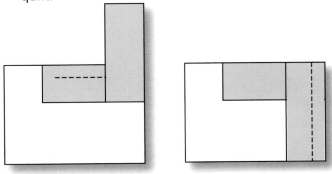

Pin in place along raw edge. Stitch along the pinned edge to the next corner. Repeat process for sewing binding to quilt, stopping approximately 10" from the starting point.

Bring the beginning and end of binding to the center of the opening and fold each end back, leaving 1/4" between the folds. Finger press the folds.

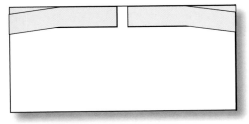

Unfold the ends of the binding and draw a line across the wrong side in the crease. Draw a line lengthwise in the pressed fold to create a cross mark. Now draw a 45- degree diagonal mark through the cross mark.

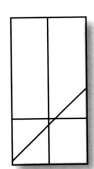 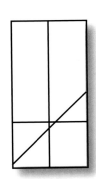

Match right sides and diagonal lines, pin binding endings together at right angles and stitch on the line.

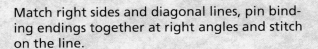

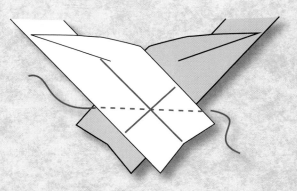

Trim the seam to 1/4" seam allowance and finger press open. Stitch to the quilt.

When you stitch the 1/4" seam allowance (which actually uses 1/2" since you have doubled the binding), you will have 1/2" left to pull around and stitch to the back side. The idea is for the batting to completely fill the binding. It looks better and it wears better. Just remember that the binding should be filled with the quilt edge. In other words, it should feel stuffed.

Turn the binding to the backside of the quilt and blindstitch in place. Fold binding over to quilt backing along one edge, covering the stitching line. On adjacent side, fold binding to make a mitered corner. Use thread that matches the binding fabric.

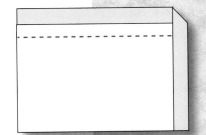 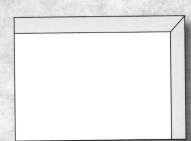

LABELS

A label is the finishing touch to your quilt. It gives you, the maker, the opportunity to give credit to all those involved in the quilt's creation. You can add the information with embroidery, appliqué, a permanent marking pen, photo transfer methods or computer generated labels. I recommend putting the following on all your labels:

- The name of the quilt
- Size of quilt
- Name of pattern (especially if it is a copyrighted pattern or from a book)
- Your name as the maker
- Name of quilter (individual or group)
- Name of recipient (if it is a gift)
- Anything of interest about the quilt

I have started adding the type of batting used.

JEANNE'S QUILT LABEL METHOD

Print all of the information in a word document on the computer. Center it on the page.

Place a preprinted label or a piece of 200-count white or off-white fabric directly over the printed page and tape in place. Put the paper back in the computer printer and run it through.

Remove the fabric label from the paper. Heat-set the printing by first pressing the fabric from the wrong side (put a pressing cloth on your ironing board so the ink will not transfer to your cover). Turn the label over, place the pressing cloth on top of the label and again press with the hot iron.

Trim the fabric, add a border if you wish and then turn the edges under. Blindstitch it to the back of your quilt.

KANSAS SAMPLER

QUILTED BY JEANNE POORE
6" BLOCKS
FINISHED SIZE: 50" x 52"

■ FABRIC REQUIREMENTS

- Assorted background fabrics for blocks: 1/2 yard total

- Assorted blue, red, green, black and gold fabrics for block: Fat eighths (11" x 18")

- Green for outer border, binding and block piecing: 1 7/8 yards

- Tan for inner border and dividing sashing strip: 5/8 yard

- Red for setting triangles and block piecing: 1 yard

- Backing: 3 yards

- Batting: Twin size

■ CUTTING INSTRUCTIONS

GREEN

2—6" x 50" strips on the straight grain of the fabric for top and bottom border

2—6" x 40 1/2" strips on the straight grain of the fabric for side borders

6—2 to 2 1/2" x 42" rectangles for binding

TAN

6—3" x 42" rectangles for inner borders and dividing sashing

RED

5—10" squares, subcut each twice diagonally for a total of 20 side setting triangles. You will have 2 extra side setting triangles.

6—6" squares, subcut each once diagonally for 12 corner setting triangles

FABRIC SELECTION

Yardages are based on 42"-wide fabric.

The fabrics used for the majority of the quilts in this book were designed by Kansas quilt makers Barbara Brackman, Terry Thompson and Lynne Hagmeier. Some of the Golden Oldies, however, chose to use their own color and fabric selections. The supply list for the finished quilt instructions uses the Kansas fabric collections.

■ INSTRUCTIONS FOR SETTING BLOCKS INTO QUILT

I recommend that you have a design wall or a large area where you can lay out the blocks in rows so you can decide the best placement from the perspective of color and movement in the overall design. When you have made your decision, then piece as follows:

Stitch the side and corner triangles to the blocks in strips as diagrammed. These setting triangles are oversized to allow for trimming of the sides to a 1/2" seam allowance. This ensures that you do not lose the points of the blocks in the seam allowance.

DO NOT trim the top and bottom edge of the strip yet. Repeat to make 2 more strips. Measure the length of the pieced strips and trim to the same length.

Trim 4 sashing/inner border strips to the length of the pieced strips. Pin the middle of the cut strips to the middle of the pieced strips; pin the ends, then pin the remaining areas, easing in any fullness. Press toward the sashing/inner border strips.

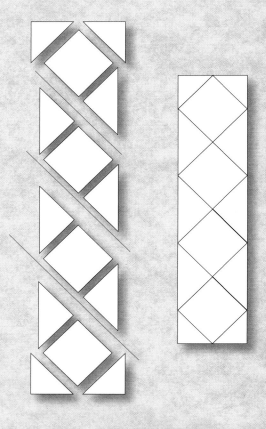

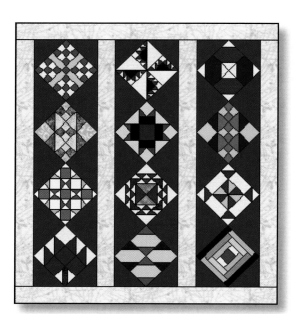

Measure from side to side across the width of the center of the quilt and at the top and bottom. Cut the 2 remaining inner border strips to the measured length. Pin in place and stitch.

■ Repeat the measuring of the quilt, this time from the top to the bottom in the center and at both sides. Cut 2 identical strips and attach as above. Press away from the quilt. Repeat to get the top and bottom measurements and stitch borders to quilt.

Quilt as desired and bind. See Basic Instructions for binding information.

IMPORTANT: Be sure to label your finished quilt. See Basic Instructions.

QUILTED BY JOAN STRECK
12" BLOCKS
FINISHED SIZE: 82" x 102"

■ FABRIC REQUIREMENTS

- Assorted background fabrics for blocks: 3 ½ yards

- Assorted blue, red, green, black and gold fabrics for blocks: 3 ½ yards
- Tan for borders, setting triangles and corner blocks: 5 yards
- Green for block framing, corner blocks, inner border and binding: 2 ¼ yards
- Backing: 6 yards
- Batting: Queen size

■ CUTTING INSTRUCTIONS

TAN

5—21 ½" squares. Subcut each diagonally twice for 20 large setting triangles.

4—11" squares. Subcut each diagonally once for 8 corner setting triangles.

Note: The following lengths should be cut after you have pieced the blocks in the center of the quilt.

2—2 ½"x 83 ½" strips along the lengthwise grain of fabric for side inner borders

2—2 ½" x 60" strips along the lengthwise grain of fabric for inner top and bottom inner border

4—2 ½" x 85 ½" strips along the lengthwise grain of fabric for flying geese side borders

4—2 ½"x 66" strips along the longwise grain of fabric for flying geese top and bottom borders

GREEN

18—1 ½" strips for pieced block framing. Subcut into 24 rectangles 1 ½" x 12 ½" and 24 rectangles 1 ½" x 14 ½".

9—1 ½" strips for inner border

10—2 ¼" strips for binding

■ BLOCKS FOR PIECED OUTER BORDER

ASSORTED PRINTS FOR FLYING GEESE
152—2 1/2" x 4 1/2" rectangles

ASSORTED BACKGROUND PRINTS FOR GEESE
304—2 1/2" squares. Draw a diagonal line on the
    wrong side of each square.

TAN FOR FRIENDSHIP STARS
8—2 7/8" squares. Draw a diagonal line on the
    wrong side of each square

4—2 1/2" squares

8—1 1/2" x 6 1/2" rectangles

8—1 1/2" x 8 1/2" rectangles

GREEN FOR FRIENDSHIP STARS
8—2 7/8" squares
16—2 1/2" squares

■ PIECING INSTRUCTIONS

CENTER OF QUILT

Arrange your blocks in vertical rows to determine
placement before stitching them together. A
design wall is beneficial, but often we do not have
the room for one. If you do not have a design wall,
look through a camera lens to see if you are satisfied
with arrangement.

In this quilt, 2 of the blocks are cut so only half is
showing in the quilt's center vertical row. DO NOT
cut the blocks in half. You must cut them so that
you have the 1/4" seam allowance on the cut edge.

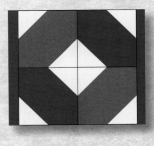

FRAMING THE BLOCKS

Stitch the 1 1/2" x 12 1/2" rectangles on opposite sides
of the 11 whole blocks. Press toward the green fabric.
Stitch the 1 1/2" x 14 1/2" rectangles on the remaining
sides of the 11 whole blocks. Press toward the green
fabric.

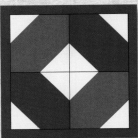

Now stitch a 1 ½" x 12 ½" rectangle on one side of a half block, then stitch the 1 ½" x 14 ½" rectangle on the adjacent side. Repeat for the other half-block.

Stitch the side and corner triangles to the row of blocks as diagrammed.

Stitch the vertical rows together, being careful to match the center of the large setting triangles to the corners of the blocks in the side rows and to have the top and bottom edges matching.

■ First border and second inner borders

Note: Be sure to measure the center of the quilt before adding each border unit. The following are the measurements for Joan's quilt, but yours may be different.

Stitch the top and bottom inner-border 2 1/2" x 60" tan strips to the quilt center.
Then add the 2 side 2 1/2" x 83 1/2" tan strips to the sides of the center.

Stitch 2 each of the green 1 1/2" strips together with a diagonal seam. Press the seam open. Trim 2 of the strips to the width of the quilt center. Stitch to the top and bottom of the quilt. Then add the 2 remaining strips to the sides of the quilt.

■ Outer border

Corner Friendship Stars

Lay the 8 tan 2 7/8" squares onto the 8 green 2 7/8" squares, right sides together. Stitch 1/2" on both sides of the drawn line. Cut on the line. Press toward the green.

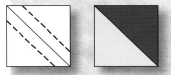

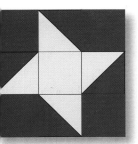

Stitch half-square triangles and green squares together in rows as diagrammed.

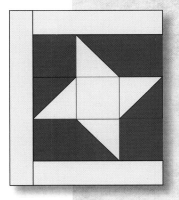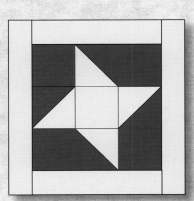

Stitch the 1 1/2" x 6 1/2" rectangles to the top and bottom of the block. Press toward the rectangles. Stitch the 1 1/2" x 8 1/2" rectangles to the sides. Press toward the rectangles.

■ FLYING GEESE UNITS

Lay a 2 1/2" background square onto one end of a 2 1/2" x 4 1/2" print rectangle, right sides together. Stitch on the line. Trim to 1/4" seam allowance. Press toward the background triangle.

Lay another 2 1/2" background square onto the other end of the rectangle, right sides together. Stitch on drawn line. Trim and press toward the triangle again. Make a total of 152 flying geese from the assorted background and print fabrics.

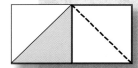 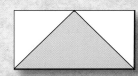

Stitch the geese together in rows as diagrammed. You should have approximately 33 units in the top and bottom rows and 43 in the side rows. Measure the width of the center of the quilt from side to side. Your top and bottom strip of flying geese and 2 1/2" tan border strips should be the same measurement: 66". Stitch geese and tan strips together as diagrammed and stitch to quilt.

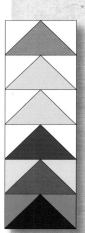 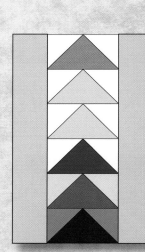

Measure the quilt again, this time from top to bottom, including the top and bottom flying geese border unit. Join the side 2 1/2" tan border strips (85 1/2") to the flying geese strips for the side borders. Add the friendship star blocks to the ends of the side border strips.

Quilt as desired and bind.
See Basic Instructions for binding information.
Note: Be sure to label your finished quilt.
See Basic Instructions

One Piece at a Time by Kansas City Star Books (1999)

More Kansas City Star Quilts by Kansas City Star Books (2000)

Outside the Box: Hexagon Patterns from The Kansas City Star by Edie McGinnis (2001)

Prairie Flower: A Year on the Plains by Barbara Brackman (2001)

The Sister Blocks by Edie McGinnis (2001)

Kansas City Quilt Makers by Doug Worgul (2001)

O Glory: Americana Quilts Blocks from The Kansas City Star by Edie McGinnis (2001)

Hearts & Flowers: Hand Applique from Start to Finish by Kathy Delaney (2002)

Roads & Curves Ahead by Edie McGinnis (2002)

Celebration of American Life: Applique Patterns Honoring a Nation and Its People by Barb Adams and Alma Allen (2002)

Women of Grace & Charm: A Quilting Tribute to the Women Who Served in World War II by Barb Adams and Alma Allen (2003)

A Heartland Album: More Techniques in Hand Applique by Kathy Delaney (2003)

Quilting a Poem: Designs Inspired by America's Poets by Frances Kite and Debra Rowden (2003)

Carolyn's Paper Pieced Garden: Patterns for Miniature and Full-Sized Quilts by Carolyn Cullinan McCormack (2003)

Friendships in Bloom: Round Robin Quilts by Marjorie Nelson and Rebecca Nelson-Zerfas (2003)

Baskets of Treasures: Designs Inspired by Life Along the River by Edie McGinnis (2003)

Heart & Home: Unique American Women and the Houses that Inspire by Kathy Schmitz (2003)

Women of Design: Quilts in the Newspaper by Barbara Brackman (2004)

The Basics: An Easy Guide to Beginning Quiltmaking by Kathy Delaney (2004)

Four Block Quilts: Echoes of History, Pieced Boldly & Appliqued Freely by Terry Clothier Thompson (2004)

No Boundaries: Bringing Your Fabric Over the Edge by Edie McGinnis (2004)

Horn of Plenty for a New Century by Kathy Delaney (2004)

Quilting the Garden by Barb Adams and Alma Allen (2004)

Stars All Around Us: Quilts and Projects Inspired by a Beloved Symbol by Cherie Ralston (2005)

Quilters' Stories: Collecting History in the Heart of America by Debra Rowden (2005)

Libertyville: Where Liberty Dwells, There is My Country by Terry Clothier Thompson (2005)

Sparkling Jewels, Pearls of Wisdom by Edie McGinnis (2005)

Grapefruit Juice & Sugar by Jenifer Dick (2005)

Home Sweet Home by Barb Adams and Alma Allen (2005)

Patterns of History: The Challenge Winners by Kathy Delaney (2005)

My Quilt Stories by Debra Rowden (2005)

Quilts in Red and Green and the Women Who Made Them by Nancy Horback and Terry Clothier Thompson (2006)

Hard Times, Splendid Quilts: A 1930s Celebration, Paper Piecing from The Kansas City Star by Carolyn Cullinan McCormick (2006)

Art Nouveau Quilts for the 21st Century by Bea Oglesby (2006)

Designer Quilts: Great Projects from Moda's Best Fabric Artists (2006)

Birds of a Feather by Barb Adams and Alma Allen (2006)

Feedsacks! Beautiful Quilts from Humble Beginnings by Edie McGinnis (2006)

Kansas Spirit: Historical Quilt Blocks and the Saga of the Sunflower State by Jeanne Poore (2006)

Queen Bees Mysteries

Murders on Elderberry Road by Sally Goldenbaum (2003)

A Murder of Taste by Sally Goldenbaum (2004)

Murder on a Starry Night by Sally Goldenbaum (2005)

Project Books

Fan Quilt Memories by Jeanne Poore (2000)

Santa's Parade of Nursery Rhymes by Jeanne Poore (2001)